W9-AET-961

FIRST SON AND PRESIDENT

A Creative Minds Biography

FIRST SON AND PRESIDENT

A Story about John Quincy Adams

by Beverly Gherman

illustrations by Matthew Bird

M Millbrook Press/Minneapolis

*To my father and grandfathers, scholars who taught
me to love books* —B.G.

*For Mom and Dad, with special thanks to
Lenny Goldman* —M.B.

All quoted material comes from books listed in the bibliography.

Text copyright © 2006 by Beverly Gherman
Illustrations copyright © 2006 by Matthew Bird

All rights reserved. International copyright secured. No part of this book
may be reproduced, stored in a retrieval system, or transmitted in any form or
by any means—electronic, mechanical, photocopying, recording, or
otherwise—without the prior written permission of Carolrhoda Books, Inc.,
except for the inclusion of brief quotations in an acknowledged review.

Millbrook Press
A division of Lerner Publishing Group
241 First Avenue North
Minneapolis, MN 55401 U.S.A.

Website address: www.lernerbooks.com

Library of Congress Cataloging-in-Publication Data

Gherman, Beverly.
    First son and president : a story about John Quincy Adams / by
Beverly Gherman ; illustrations by Matthew Bird.
        p.   cm. — (A creative minds biography)
    Includes bibliographical references and index.
    ISBN-13: 978–1–57505–756–9 (lib. bdg. : alk. paper)
    ISBN-10: 1–57505–756–5 (lib. bdg. : alk. paper)
    1. Adams, John Quincy, 1767–1848—Juvenile literature. 2. Presidents—
United States—Biography—Juvenile literature. I. Bird, Matthew, ill.
II. Title. III. Series.
E377.G46 2006
973.5'5'092—dc22   2004028550

Manufactured in the United States of America
1 2 3 4 5 6 – JR – 11 10 09 08 07 06

Table of Contents

High Hopes   7

Young Man Abroad   11

Student at Home   21

Foreign Minister   27

Statesman   32

Best Office in the Administration   40

President of the United States   45

At Home in the House   50

Afterword   60

Bibliography   61

Index   62

About the Author and Illustrator   64

1

High Hopes

In the middle of a June night in 1775, seven-year-old Johnny woke from a deep sleep to find his mother Abigail bending over him. He heard the deep roaring sounds of cannons and felt the house shake with each explosion.

Together, Johnny and Abigail raced from their Braintree, Massachusetts, farmhouse. They rushed through the orchards and over rock walls until they reached the top of Penn's Hill. On its huge stone ledge, they watched the flash of the cannon and the smoke of rifles from the Battle of Bunker Hill. The battle between the British and the American colonists was more than ten miles away. They were safe for the present.

Johnny's father, John Adams, was not home. He had been elected a member of the Continental Congress. The Congress, with members from all the colonies, was meeting in Philadelphia. It was discussing ways for the colonies to free themselves from British rule. John worried about the safety of his family so close to the danger of battle. "Fly to the woods," John wrote, if the British soldiers come near.

The colonists were fighting for their freedom from Great Britain and its leader, King George III. The king wanted to keep the colonies under his control. He wanted them to pay British taxes and follow British laws. Many colonists felt this was unfair.

Mother and son learned later that many men were killed that night in the Battle of Bunker Hill. Johnny must have been relieved his father was too old for battle. He was a lawyer and a politician who fought with words rather than rifles.

In the following days, Abigail opened their small home to families who had lost their own homes in the war. One night she put up a whole troop of soldiers. Some men slept in the barn, others in the attic. In the morning, they practiced marching behind the house. Johnny joined them, pretending to shoulder his gun and match their step.

Another day he watched his mother melt down her

pewter spoons to be made into bullets. He knew both his parents felt a great sense of duty to their country. He would look for ways to serve also.

John Quincy Adams was the first son born to John and Abigail Adams on July 11, 1767. He already had a two-year-old sister, Abigail, whom they called Nabby. His brother Charles was born in 1770 and Thomas in 1772. As the oldest son, Johnny became the man of the house while his father was away. He helped his mother with the crops and the animals on their property. He took care of his younger brothers and even tried to tell his sister what she must do.

Abigail gathered all of the children around her to hear their father's frequent letters. She told them that their father could be found a traitor if the British captured him because he was fighting against British rule. He faced danger every mile of the fifteen-day journey from Braintree to Philadelphia.

Abigail taught Johnny and Nabby to read and write. A cousin who lived with them, John Thaxter, taught Johnny languages and mathematics. Johnny's father also gave him assignments in his letters. He was to study Latin and Greek. He was also to study history to learn of the many evils that had occurred in the past. This would help him make good choices in the future.

Visiting Boston, on July 18, 1776, Abigail and nine-year-old Johnny heard the Declaration of Independence read from the balcony of the statehouse. The Declaration stated that the American colonies were no longer part of Great Britain. Johnny's father had helped Thomas Jefferson and others write the Declaration, and Johnny must have felt pride in hearing the powerful words:

> We . . . declare, that these United Colonies are, and of Right ought to be Free and Independent States.

Once the reading ended, the hushed crowd cheered. Bells rang. British flags were taken down and burned. Even though Johnny was young, he must have known that history was being made during those times of war and change.

From the earliest days, his parents treated Johnny like an adult. One of his jobs was to ride his horse the ten rugged miles between Braintree and Boston to get the mail, even though the fighting continued in that city. He worried that British soldiers might be hidden behind every tree, waiting to capture him. But it was his way to serve.

2

Young Man Abroad

The new United States hoped that France would help them fight the British. The Continental Congress asked John Adams to represent the U.S. government in Paris, France. Adams accepted, even though Paris was far away and he would be gone a long time. When Johnny heard the news, he begged to go too.

Johnny and his father left in February 1778, aboard the new twenty-four-gun ship, the *Boston*. Neither of them had ever sailed before. Abigail sent them off with enough supplies for a voyage of many weeks.

She included chickens, two sheep, fresh meat, four-teen dozen eggs, five bushels of corn, a barrel of apples, thirty pounds of sugar, two pounds of tea, and large hunks of chocolate.

The first day at sea, the weather was calm and Johnny began learning French from a surgeon in the French army. On the second day, British ships were sighted and a chase began. "Sometimes we gained upon her, sometimes she upon us," John Adams wrote. It took two more days for the captain to escape from the enemy. Then the weather changed.

Battering winds and high waves attacked the ship. The main mast split in half. No one could stand on deck. Lightning struck and killed one of the men. In their shared cabin, Johnny and his father were both seasick. The ship leaked. Their food, their clothing, their papers were soaked by enormous waves.

After several days, the storm passed. John wrote Abigail that their son "behaves like a man," working with the sailors, practicing his French, studying his books, despite all the difficulties they experienced. The captain was also impressed with Johnny's brav-ery. On calm days, he taught Johnny how to adjust the sails and keep the ship going in the right direction. Johnny drew detailed pictures of ships and could name each of the sails.

It was April when at last they landed in Bordeaux, France. There, Johnny ate his first French food and found its rich sauces tastier than the plain meals he was used to at home. He agreed with his father that "this is a delicious Country."

They traveled by coach several more days to reach Paris. John's friend, Benjamin Franklin, was already in France serving the new American government. Franklin had been a scientist and printer in Philadelphia. He had spent years in Britain and France working for the American colonies and the new United States. He had a home in Passy, a village outside Paris, and he invited John and Johnny to stay with him.

Johnny was sent to boarding school, where he studied Latin and French. He studied fencing, or sword fighting, and took dancing lessons and drawing and music classes. The school day began in the early morning and continued until eight thirty in the evening. Johnny was already able to speak some French, so he fit in with the other boys right away.

On weekends he stayed with his father, and together they dined out and attended musical programs and theater. John was discouraged because he could not keep up with his son's language skills. "This child . . . learned more French in a day than I could learn in a Week with all my books," he wrote.

John's work in France ended after a year, and he and Johnny sailed for home in June 1779. On the ship, Johnny taught English to the new French representative to the United States and his secretary. His proud father wrote to Abigail that the representative thought their son was as good as a professor.

Crossing the Atlantic on their return trip was much easier than it had been eighteen months earlier. The weather was calm, and they were not chased by British ships. But it was the first voyage with all its fear and excitement that they would never forget.

They were home in Braintree for only three months when John was asked to return to Paris to help write treaties with Great Britain and France. This time, Johnny didn't want to go. But Abigail felt it was important for twelve-year-old Johnny and his nine-year-old brother Charles to be with their father. They needed his guidance and supervision.

The three of them left on November 13, 1779. Saying good-bye to his mother, Charley couldn't stop crying. He was not as confident as his older brother had been on his first voyage.

On this voyage, Johnny took his father's advice to keep a diary of daily events and the people he met. That December he began his journal, writing on the first page, "a journal By Me JQA."

This time, they lived in Paris. Johnny again went to school in Passy, and Charles joined him there. They were required to study Latin and Greek, geography, mathematics, drawing, and writing.

Johnny's interest in the French theater continued. He wrote his mother that he had fallen in love with a young actress whom he was eager to meet. He thought she was fourteen and was the "most lovely and delightful actress that I ever saw."

Abigail worried about her son being exposed to a life so different from the sheltered life he might have led in Braintree. But she had other worries as well. The British army continued to raid towns and villages near Braintree. Fighting had also moved to the southern states. The British still hoped to defeat the United States.

On July 27, 1780, John took his sons to Amsterdam in Holland. He hoped the Dutch would support American independence and even give the colonies a loan. America had many debts from the long war with Britain.

Johnny was to study at the University of Leyden, about thirty miles away, and both boys were to live with their cousin, John Thaxter. Johnny wrote frequently to his father. He told his father that the university was considered one of the finest in the world. He also wrote that he was learning a great deal from the lectures. He and Charles were studying with a teacher as well.

In one letter Johnny asked for a pair of skates and riding pants and boots. His father agreed that he should have what he needed for riding and skating but that he should not spend too much time on such amusements. And his mother wrote, telling Johnny he should learn to be as neat and clean as the country in which he lived.

In April 1781, Charles returned to Braintree with a family friend. Charles had been ill with a fever and was too homesick to stay away longer.

That July, when Johnny was fourteen, he went to Russia. Francis Dana had been named American minister to the government of the Russian empress Catherine the Great. He hoped to sign a formal agreement between America and Russia. Members of the Russian court spoke French. Johnny's French would be helpful to Dana, who spoke only English. He would serve as Dana's secretary.

In those days, Russia was a large, unknown country. Johnny and Dana traveled two thousand miles by coach. They went through Germany and Poland and traveled north in Russia until they reached Saint Petersburg, the capital at the time. Johnny thought it the most beautiful city he had ever seen.

After all their efforts, Catherine the Great was not interested in meeting with Francis Dana and his young secretary. There was no school for Johnny to attend, because most royal children were educated in France. He began studying German on his own.

After fifteen months, his father told him to return to Amsterdam because he needed Johnny to serve as his secretary. John also sent a long list of things Johnny must do. He should keep details of his travels in his journal. He should study his Latin and Greek and mathematics. He should treat people he met with great respect. And he should not spend too much money.

Johnny left Russia on October 30, 1782, and traveled through Sweden, Norway, Denmark, and northern Germany. He didn't arrive in Holland until April 1783. Johnny had often traveled alone, and everywhere he went, he was treated well. He was a friendly, intelligent young man who could speak many languages. Johnny had grown up, and his travels had been an important part of his education.

At last, he joined his father. John was on the committee meeting with the British to work out a treaty to end the war. They signed the Treaty of Paris in August 1783. As secretary, Johnny took notes of the meetings and made copies of the papers. He was present at another important moment in history.

John Adams was asked to stay on in France to work on trade agreements. He sent for his wife and daughter to join him. The younger boys stayed with Abigail's sister in Massachusetts.

When Abigail arrived in Paris and saw Johnny, she could hardly recognize the handsome young man standing before her. He had been a boy when he left six years earlier. Now he was almost eighteen.

John Quincy and his sister became good friends. Nabby was twenty by then and eager to see all the sights of Paris. Johnny was glad to show them to her.

When they weren't exploring the museums and gardens, the family spent time planning John Quincy's future. They all agreed it was time for him to return to the United States. He needed to complete his education at Harvard College, where his father had been a student.

John Quincy wasn't sure. He liked the life he led in Europe. He wrote in his diary about his worry over returning to a small college in Massachusetts after having attended the "noble" University of Leyden. But he was given no choice.

3

Student at Home

John Quincy left Paris by ship in May 1785. His heavy trunks were packed with clothing, bed linen, and books. Heaviest of all were his parents' words. They reminded him that he must put his "carefree years abroad behind him."

He celebrated his eighteenth birthday on the ship. The following week, John Quincy arrived in New York City. From there, he traveled by horseback to Braintree. He visited his mother's sister, Mary Cranch. Everyone was amazed by the handsome young man he had become and by the fluent French he spoke. They admired his many stories and his European clothes. He had sixty-five pairs of stockings, four pairs of shoes, and coats and suits, all in blue or black.

John Quincy met with Joseph Willard, the president of Harvard. Willard told him he needed to study more before he could enter the college. His Latin and Greek were not as good as they should be. John Quincy had left Europe a confident young man. Now he was crushed. He went to live in nearby Haverhill with his uncle and aunt, John and Elizabeth Shaw. His uncle taught him through the winter.

In March a less cocky John Quincy appeared before the entire Harvard teaching staff: Joseph Willard, four tutors, three professors, and the librarian. After John Quincy finished the examination, they asked him to wait while they met together.

John Quincy waited nervously for what seemed like hours while they reached their decision. But after only fifteen minutes, they called him back. President Willard said Harvard would accept him, but he had to work hard to keep up. He could enter as a third-year student, just as his father had requested.

John was not always a great student. Sometimes he missed classes because he overslept after a late night of partying. But he loved his books and the ideas they held. He was invited to join a literary society. The members wrote essays and read them to each other. He saw that he was good at writing essays and hoped with practice he would get better at presenting them.

After fifteen months at Harvard, John Quincy graduated in July 1787. He was ranked second highest in a class of fifty-one. He gave the graduation speech and was asked to become a member of Phi Beta Kappa, a new organization to honor the brightest students.

He and his cousin Billy Cranch graduated at the same time. Billy's mother, John's Aunt Mary, prepared a feast of roast chicken and roast beef, boiled ham, tongue, and a huge plum cake for dessert. She rented two large rooms at Harvard and invited the whole family to celebrate.

John Quincy's parents were still in London. After many weeks, he received a letter from them telling him how proud they were. But they also reminded him to study and work hard "for your country will one day call for your services."

School was over for John. He worried about how he would make a living. His parents could not afford to support him forever. The family had decided that he would study law as his father had. That meant becoming an apprentice to a lawyer.

John Quincy chose to study with Theophilus Parsons in Newburyport, a seaport town fifty miles northeast of Boston. John quickly made friends and attended parties in Newburyport. He also tried to learn the rules of law.

In the summer of 1788, his parents returned from Britain. John Quincy joined them in Braintree and helped them settle into their house. They both told him how proud they were of all his accomplishments.

In 1789 George Washington was elected president of the country. John Quincy's father was to be vice president. They would head the new government in New York the following year.

In July of 1790, John Quincy opened a law office in Boston. As he sat waiting through the summer for clients, he read his favorite books and wrote poetry and essays about the new government.

John Quincy did not put his name on the essays but called them "Letters of Publicola," Latin for "friend of the people." He wrote about his belief in a strong federal government that made laws to govern all the states. He thought there should be a national bank to pay the government's debts. His father and others agreed with this idea. They were called Federalists.

Republicans, including such leaders as Thomas Jefferson, believed in the rights of each individual. They wanted the states, not the federal government, to protect those rights. They felt a national bank controlled by the government took power from the states. This issue divided the people and led to the beginning of political parties.

In 1793, John Quincy wrote another group of essays under the name of Marcellus, and many people began to realize who the author was. In these essays, he said that the United States should stay neutral in the war that had begun between France and Great Britain.

After the slow summer, John Quincy tried his first case as a lawyer in October 1793. When he went into court, he was so nervous he could not speak well, and his thoughts were not well organized. He lost the case. He worried that he wasn't meant to be a lawyer.

Over the next few years, his law practice grew slowly, and he won more cases than he lost. He also continued to write political essays. By the spring of 1794, John Quincy told his father, "I find myself contented with my state as it is." He was becoming well known both as a lawyer and as a political essayist.

4

Foreign Minister

In June 1794, President George Washington appointed John Quincy minister to Holland. He was to represent the United States in that country. At first, John Quincy worried that he was chosen just because his father had recommended him for the job. But Vice President Adams said that was not true. John didn't mention that he had shared his son's Publicola essays with the president.

Then John Quincy worried that he might not be old enough and wise enough for such a post. He was not yet twenty-seven. Still, he decided to accept the position. He bought himself a new diary in which to record his experiences, and he began reading the records written by past ministers.

John Quincy asked his younger brother Thomas to serve as his secretary. They arrived in Holland in November. After six months, he wrote in his diary how pleased he was to be working there.

In November 1795, John Quincy was asked to take papers to Joshua Johnson, a U.S. official in London. Johnson had seven daughters, and John Quincy went back to the Johnsons quite often. He especially liked Louisa, their second daughter. She spoke French and could talk with him on every subject.

Louisa was a spirited young woman. John Quincy made the mistake of telling Mrs. Johnson that he hoped to marry her daughter without first asking Louisa. She was furious. At first, she refused even to see John Quincy. Eventually, she agreed to marry him and wanted to set a date. By then he was having second thoughts and worried he was not ready for marriage. He returned to Holland at the end of May 1796 without setting any date.

In early 1797, John Quincy learned that his father had been elected the second president of the United States. John Quincy was to serve as the first representative to the kingdom of Prussia, a country that is now part of Germany. He told Louisa they must postpone their marriage, but she said she would not wait a moment longer. They must marry so that she could go with him.

On the morning of July 26, John Quincy and Louisa Catherine were married in the parish church at All Hallows Barking. He was thirty; she was twenty-two.

They were a handsome couple, but they had very different natures. Louisa was outgoing, loved music, and played both the harp and the piano. John Quincy was a loner and a worrier and much more serious than his lively wife. He needed time alone for his writing.

He and Louisa left for Berlin, the capital of Prussia, in the fall. At first, John Quincy felt himself a stranger. His German was not good enough for conversation, and he didn't know anyone in Prussia. But in just a few weeks, he was welcomed by the new king, Frederick William III, and his ministers. Soon he was speaking German as though he were a native. Louisa enjoyed the formal banquets and balls and was comfortable planning their social events. Their lives were filled with concerts, theater, and art.

Louisa and John Quincy's first son was born in Berlin on April 12, 1801. They called him George Washington Adams. To celebrate his son's arrival, John rose at six o'clock and walked three miles for a swim in the Spree River.

Several weeks later, he learned that his father had lost the election in 1800 to Thomas Jefferson. The new president would choose his own staff to represent the government. This meant John Quincy was called back to the United States. John Quincy was not happy about giving up the life he and Louisa had led. He knew that he would have to find a new one in the United States. The three of them sailed for home in July 1801. John Quincy had been in Europe for seven years.

Louisa was nervous about meeting her mother-in-law. And Abigail didn't try to hide her disapproval of Louisa. She thought of her as a "frail and fancy" woman and called her a "half-blood" because her mother was British. But John Adams welcomed his daughter-in-law warmly. John Quincy, Louisa, and the baby had to stay with his parents until their own house in Boston was ready in December.

As they settled into their new home, John Quincy's head was filled with worries. He worried about how he was to support his wife and child. He worried that he would have to give up his favorite activities, reading history and writing political essays. His parents had decided John Quincy should continue with his law practice and not think of a political career. Years earlier he had said he "would rather clean filth from the streets of Boston than be a politician."

5

Statesman

John Quincy finally accepted the fact that he could earn a living by working in a "dreary" law practice during the day. He made up for it in the evenings by meeting with interesting friends. With them he formed the Natural Philosophy Club. Together they performed scientific experiments and discussed books and political ideas. After a year, though, he was ready for a change.

John Quincy decided that, rather than being a politician, he would be a statesman. Being a statesman meant being a leader by making wise decisions without taking the side of one political party or another. He wanted to be the "man of [his] whole country."

He became a state senator in Massachusetts in 1802. He wrote in his journal at the end of the year that he was pleased he had been able to remain independent in that office.

By February 1803, John Quincy was elected by the legislature to serve as a U.S. senator for a six-year term. While he was preparing for his new role by reading about the history of the country, Louisa gave birth to their second son on July 4, 1803.

They named him John Adams II, in honor of his grandfather. The whole family moved to Washington, D.C., which had become the capital of the United States.

John Quincy's day began with reading and writing before breakfast. He ate at nine o'clock and then walked to the Capitol building. He timed his walk with his pocket watch, noting that it took him forty-five minutes. In those days, the Senate met from noon until two or three in the afternoon. He was home every day for dinner at four o'clock.

The Adamses quickly became part of Washington society. They were invited to all the dinners and balls. In the evenings, when they were not out for social events, Adams worked on his papers by candlelight until late at night.

John Quincy was not as popular with his fellow senators. He worked hard to understand the issues. Then he voted as he thought right, regardless of party politics. Often his vote was the opposite of the votes of the other New England senators.

He supported President Jefferson's bill to add the Louisiana Purchase land to the United States. This area, bought from France, doubled the size of the United States. But he fought against Jefferson's plan to set the boundary between British-owned Canada and the United States. He didn't want to give Great Britain a large strip of the land claimed by the United States.

The Senate sessions were over in the late spring. Soon after, the Adams family left Washington for Braintree, which had been renamed Quincy. John and Abigail had given them the farmhouse in which John Quincy had been born and the land surrounding it. The young family would make that farmhouse their temporary home.

In June 1805, John Quincy was asked to be a professor of rhetoric and oratory at Harvard, teaching students how to write and speak well. He told the new president of the university that he planned to keep his Senate seat, even though it required a great deal of his time. He was certain he could do both.

In mid-June, he was installed as a new professor in a formal ceremony on Harvard's campus in Cambridge. Wearing a heavy woolen academic robe, he suffered terribly on that muggy day. But he was determined to prove that he could give a good lecture.

He taught his first class on July 11, his thirty-ninth birthday, and he thought that it was one of the best days of his life.

For four years, he traveled back and forth from Washington and the Senate to Quincy and Harvard. Improved roadways for coaches made travel time much faster than it had been. It used to take fifteen days to travel to Philadephia from Quincy. He could make a similar trip from Quincy to Washington, D.C., in about two days.

That first summer and autumn, he gave a lecture on Friday mornings, and in the afternoon, he became the audience and listened to the students recite. At first, only a few students attended his lectures or showed up to recite before him.

After several months, the lecture room was nearly full, and the students' talks had improved greatly. Louisa gave birth to their third son, Charles Francis Adams, on August 17, 1807.

In June 1808, John Quincy resigned from the Senate. He knew he would not win re-election. The people at home were angry because he had not always voted the way they wanted. He chose to spend his time with four young students who were reading law with him. He also continued teaching his students at Harvard, and he made time to speak French with his son George.

The newly elected president, James Madison, asked John Quincy to represent the United States in Russia. Though he was sorry to leave his Harvard classes, John and Louisa left on August 5, 1809. They took two-year-old Charles Francis with them. The two older boys stayed with his parents in Quincy.

It had been twenty years since he had been in Russia, and during that earlier stay, he had never met the empress. This time, John Quincy was welcomed by the emperor, Czar Alexander. Together they walked along the banks of the Neva River in Saint Petersburg, speaking in French. The czar and his wife, Princess Elizabeth, often invited the Adamses to visit the palace. They had no children and loved to play with two-year-old Charles Francis.

John Quincy wrote often to his sons at home telling them to work hard, just as his parents had told him in their letters when he was apart from them. When Charles was four, John Quincy began teaching him, but Charles was too young to sit still for serious learning.

Louisa gave birth to their first daughter on August 11, 1811. They named the child Louisa Catherine.

The little girl brought them great joy until her first birthday. Then she became ill and died. In their grief, John Quincy and Louisa could hardly face each other or their friends.

In August 1812, they learned that a war between the United States and Great Britain had been declared three months earlier. The United States was fighting to stop British attacks on U.S. ships and to protect northern forts along the Canadian border. In 1814 the British captured Washington, D.C., and set fire to the President's House.

President Madison chose John Quincy and two others to travel to Ghent, Belgium, to work out a peace treaty between Britain and the United States. Louisa and Charles remained in Russia. For months the representatives from both countries fought over the terms of the treaty. Finally, on Christmas Eve 1814, they agreed on the terms to end the War of 1812.

John Quincy wrote Louisa faithfully from Ghent. He confided to her that President Madison would soon name him U.S. minister to Great Britain. He advised her to sell their furniture. Then she should meet him in Paris.

Louisa and Charles met John Quincy in Paris, then traveled on to Great Britain. There, they found fourteen-year-old George and eleven-year-old John waiting for them. Their sons had sailed from Massachusetts with friends of the family. They said that grandfather John Adams had told them to keep diaries, just as he had told their father when he first traveled.

John Quincy planned to work with George on his studies, while Charles and John went to a school nearby. George was not a willing student, but John Quincy was mellowing. "We must be content to take children for children," he wrote in his diary.

John Quincy was happier in those years in Great Britain than he had ever been. His whole family was with him. He had accepted his sons' limitations. He had time to think and to write and had begun writing poetry. He wrote when sitting for his portrait, during sermons, and during the night when he couldn't sleep. He knew he wasn't a great poet, but that didn't stop him. He wrote poems in honor of his friends, he wrote love poetry to Louisa, and he wrote poetry about his own desires.

He wrote in his diary, "Could I have chosen my own genius and condition, I should have made myself a great poet."

6

Best Office in the Administration

In April 1817, John Quincy received a letter from the new president, James Monroe. The letter asked him to serve as secretary of state. In this position, he would be in charge of all international interests of the United States. First, he worried, as he always did, that the job would take all of his time. It would force him to give up poetry, reading, and working with his children. But he had been called to serve, and he could not refuse. Besides, he knew it was "the best office in the . . . administration." He would be using his knowledge of foreign countries to benefit the United States.

The family left Great Britain on June 15, 1817. Adams celebrated his fiftieth birthday aboard ship. All the passengers, even those from below deck, brought him good wishes.

When they reached Quincy that August, the older boys raced to hug their grandparents, whom they had missed greatly. This time, both Abigail and John gave all of them, including Louisa, a warm welcome. They had been away nearly eight years, and Abigail's concerns about her daughter-in-law seemed to have been forgotten.

John Quincy's first goal was to find schools for the boys. George was accepted at Harvard, and the younger boys would attend a private school in Boston.

Louisa and John Quincy traveled on to Washington. They found a rented house, and John Quincy met with President Monroe. He had many things to accomplish in his new job. One of his tasks was to work on a treaty between Great Britain and the United States. It would settle the midwestern boundary between the United States and Canada.

John Quincy worked so hard he and Louisa could not get away to spend the whole summer in Quincy. They did manage to spend a few weeks there in late August. Shortly after they returned to Washington,

Abigail came down with a serious disease, typhoid fever. She seemed to be getting well and then suddenly died on October 28, 1818. By the time John Quincy learned about her death, the funeral already had taken place. He wrote a long, loving letter to his father about how much his mother had always meant to him—how she had always urged him to do his very best. He wanted to rush to his father's side in Quincy, but he could not leave his responsibilities for the United States' foreign affairs.

Even though he was grieving, he walked down to the old sycamore tree on the bank of the Potomac River as he always did each morning before work. He left all his clothes on the ground and went for a swim in the river. Then he dressed and went to his office.

One of John Quincy's most important contributions as secretary of state was his report on weights and measures. He had been studying Europe's standards for measuring distances and weights, and he felt the new United States should have the same standards. He wanted to adopt the French metric system, which is based on the number ten. But the United States finally chose the system that uses the pound and the mile instead. His report is still remarkable, even after more than two hundred years. His father thought it was too long and filled with too many facts.

He also wrote a paper describing his thoughts on foreign policy for President Monroe. Later, the president used John's ideas in his speech to Congress. John Quincy complained that the president had taken the best parts, "the cream of my paper," to use as his own.

In his paper, he recommended that the United States respect the boundaries of European colonies in the Americas. But he warned these countries against taking more land or creating new colonies in North or South America. At that time, Spain was threatening to take over free South American countries in which it used to have colonies centuries before. John advised that the United States should act independently and warn Europe that it would not permit this. These recommendations became known as the Monroe Doctrine, but John Quincy knew he had written them.

7

President of the United States

During his second term as secretary of state, John Quincy began to think about the future. Often a secretary of state went on to become president. He thought he would make a good president. He knew he would have competition from Andrew Jackson, a popular general and war hero from Tennessee.

John Quincy hoped he could persuade Jackson to run as his vice president. He and Louisa planned an elaborate ball for the general. Everyone wore their finest clothing, and it was a festive evening. It was said that one thousand guests attended the party. Some guests had to stand on chairs in order to see General Jackson entering with Louisa on his arm.

The general enjoyed the ball, but afterward, he told John Quincy he still wanted to run for president. Both of them began to campaign. So did Speaker of the House Henry Clay from Kentucky and the treasury secretary William Crawford of Georgia.

No candidate won a majority of the votes. That meant that the House of Representatives, part of Congress, had to choose the president. John Quincy Adams finally was notified that he had won a close election in February 1825.

The first thing John Quincy did was to write to his father, asking for his "blessings and prayers." John Adams, then ninety, wrote back, saying his son had been blessed beginning in his cradle! It was the first time a father and son both served as president in the new country. John was the second president and John Quincy, the sixth.

When John Quincy gave his first message to Congress, he told them about the dreams he had always had for the country. He wanted to establish a Department of the Interior, to watch over the vast lands that were part of the United States. He wanted to build roads, canals, and harbors to connect the parts of the country. He also wanted to create a military academy, an observatory to study the stars, and opportunities for scientific exploration.

Members of Congress were startled. Presidents did not have the right to suggest such enormous improvements, they said. He sounded like he wanted to be king, not president. But John Quincy had a broad view of the world. He had traveled and lived in many other countries where he had seen such wonders. He wanted to bring these wonders to the United States.

Living in the President's House was not easy for John Quincy or Louisa. There was no running water or indoor plumbing. Farm animals grazed on the lawns. The house needed repairs, and Congress allowed a small amount of money for repairs and improvements. Once the house was in better shape, the Adamses gave large, formal dinners for members of Congress and small dinners for old friends.

John Quincy had always enjoyed being outdoors. He learned the calls of birds near the President's House and those he heard on his horseback rides in the country. He studied the plants and trees wherever he went. He often took cuttings to transplant in the Washington garden or later in the Quincy garden.

In early July 1826, John Quincy received a letter that his father was ailing. He rushed to Quincy to be with him but was too late to see his father alive. He learned that his father and Thomas Jefferson had both died on July 4, only a few hours apart. It was the fiftieth anniversary of the signing of the Declaration of Independence.

The following year, the new Democratic Party won the most seats in Congress. These new congressmen did not believe in a strong federal government. They felt each of the states should take care of its own projects. The new Congress defeated every proposal John Quincy made.

Then Congress passed a tax, called a tariff. It raised fees on goods coming into the country. This was hard on the South. Most southerners were farmers, and the tariff raised the prices of manufactured goods they bought from other countries. The bill also raised the tariffs on raw materials needed by northern factories. It was called the "tariff of abominations," because it made everyone unhappy with the government.

Adams felt his presidency was made up of one disappointment after another. It would seem that John Quincy was a man ahead of his time. He and his ideas would not be appreciated until some future day.

8

At Home in the House

John Quincy ran for a second term as president and lost the election to his old rival, Andrew Jackson. On March 3, 1829, his last morning as president, he went to the Capitol to sign the papers on his desk and officially ended the Twentieth Congress. By nine that evening, John Quincy had left the President's House to join his family in their new home.

He and Louisa had rented a house not far from the Capitol. Louisa had been quite ill while they lived in the President's House, and she was glad to get away from it.

John Quincy was eager to get to work. His first project was a history of his political life. It would defend the choices he had made. He had finished writing it in late April, when he learned the terrible news about his son George.

George had been traveling by steamboat to meet his parents in Washington, but he never arrived. When only his cloak and hat were found on April 30, it was assumed that he had jumped from the boat. Notes were found at his home saying his life was unbearable and that he might take his own life. In his grief over the loss of his son and the presidency, John Quincy decided not to publish the long report he had just finished writing.

John Quincy and Louisa left Washington for Quincy in June. They moved into his parents home, which had been left to him. While he grieved, he tried to stay busy. He had so much to do that he hardly knew where to begin. He wanted to write his father's story. He wanted to study the family history. Then he became caught up in his father's library, studying old familiar books.

Instead of completing all the projects inside the house, John Quincy began working in his gardens. He used some of Louisa's best dishes to sprout acorns and peach and plum seeds. He even kept caterpillars in small glass containers so that he could watch them turn into butterflies. He planted tiny white oak trees, hoping they would outlive him.

Every morning he started the day swimming in Quincy Bay. He swam a mile naked except for a white nightcap to protect his head from the sun. In the afternoon, he walked to the village center and back. He was sixty-three, but he saw no reason to stop his exercise.

One day two friends came to speak with John Quincy. They wanted him to run for the House of Representatives. They told him it would be an honor for the House to have his great knowledge and experience. John Quincy responded that he would not seek the office, but if he were asked to serve, he could not refuse.

Louisa and Charles were upset. They wanted him to retire from politics and finish all the projects at home. But John was thrilled to be needed by his country again. He was nominated in mid-October, and on November 7, he was announced the winner.

When he heard the results he wrote, "I am a member of the Twenty-second Congress. . . . I have received nearly three votes in four throughout the district. My election as President of the United States was not half as gratifying to my inmost soul." John Quincy didn't mind that he was doing things backwards—becoming a representative after his presidency, rather than before.

At about this same time, his son John II became very ill. He was an alcoholic, who could not stop drinking. John II died on October 23, 1834, never recognizing that his father was with him. He was only thirty-one years old. Again, John Quincy and Louisa were heartbroken. But John Quincy forced himself to continue his work in Congress, despite his grief.

In December 1835, John Quincy learned that James Smithson, an Englishman, had left half a million dollars in gold to the United States. It was to be used for an institution to advance knowledge. It was exactly what John Quincy had hoped for when he was president, but then he could not persuade Congress to support his idea.

He was made chairman of the committee to decide how to use the gift. It took ten long years of arguing among members of Congress, but finally the money was used for founding a national museum. The Smithsonian Institution is the result of the original gift.

When John Quincy was sixty-five, a letter in a Boston newspaper described him as "looking younger and sprightlier than when he stood at the head of the nation." There was no question that the battles he fought in Congress kept him young.

Yet it was frustrating for him when he tried to discuss certain issues in the House. Slavery had been outlawed in the North, but not in the South. Most of the southern slaveholders did not want slavery brought up for discussion. The southern representatives passed a rule in 1836. This rule said that no one could discuss slavery or whether it should be ended. These representatives voted for the gag rule in every session of Congress.

John Quincy looked for ways to get around the rule. Often before the beginning of a meeting of Congress, he stood and read from letters he had received that asked that slavery be ended. Other representatives insisted he stop reading and sit down. Day after day, he read from his letters, sometimes adding his own arguments before he was silenced.

John Quincy was more popular in the northern states than he was among members of the House. When he was almost seventy, he was invited to speak on the Fourth of July in the town of Newburyport, where he had studied law. His subject was the Declaration of Independence. After his speech, long lines of admirers waited in line to shake his hand.

When he was in his seventies, he traveled by steamboat and canal boat and overland by stagecoach all the way to Cincinnati, Ohio. There he dedicated the site for an observatory to study the stars. One of his presidential dreams had come true.

In 1841 John Quincy was asked to take a case to the Supreme Court, the highest court in the United States. At first, he thought he was too old. After all, he was seventy-four. It had been more than thirty years since he had spoken before the Court. Finally, he said he would take the case. He was to represent thirty-nine Mende Africans who had been taken from their country to become slaves.

The Africans took over the ship they were on, *La Amistad,* and tried to force the sailors to return them to Africa. The sailors tricked the Africans and sailed the ship to Long Island, New York. The U.S. Navy took over the ship and jailed the Africans.

The Supreme Court would decide whether the Africans were freemen or slaves. John Quincy studied the records from the case. He read law books. He wanted to know as much as possible when he went before the judges of the Supreme Court.

He was used to giving long speeches and talked for four hours on the first day of the trial. When the Court met again, he spoke for another four hours.

He argued that the Africans were human beings who had every right to their freedom. The Declaration of Independence said so. He said that the real criminals were the captain and the crew who had taken the Africans from their homes.

Five days later, the judges agreed with John Quincy and declared the Africans free. Antislavery groups celebrated John Quincy, and the grateful African men gave him a handsome Bible that they had signed.

In 1845, he once again stood before the House and moved that the gag rule be ended. This time, he was successful. After eight years, he had succeeded in opening free debate on slavery.

When Louisa begged him to retire from politics, he said that he could not live without serving. Politics was "as much a necessary of life" as breathing, he told her.

He had become one of the hardest workers in the House of Representatives. He wrote over sixty thousand words in reports and other papers, plus letters to his son and friends at home. Everything was set down with his quill pen and ink. No wonder his fingers were always stained black.

John Quincy also liked to spend time with his grandchildren. They read the Bible with him in French and English, and he gave each of them a Bible of their own. They also studied astronomy with him and helped him plant more small trees.

John Quincy won a landslide victory to serve a seventh term in the House of Representatives in November 1846. The following July, he celebrated his eightieth birthday in Quincy with his family and the whole neighborhood. Although he was still active, he was becoming frail.

On February 21, 1848, he rose from his House seat to speak. He was unsteady and grasped the desk. As he began to fall, one representative caught him, and others came to help. They laid him on a sofa and carried him into a small room. He had suffered a stroke, and they could do nothing for him. He said farewell to his old friend Henry Clay before slipping into a coma. Louisa rushed to his side, but he never woke again.

John Quincy Adams died on February 23, 1848, at 7:15 P.M. Thousands of people came to pay their respects to him while his body lay in state in the Capitol. Two days later, a funeral train carried his coffin accompanied by members of Congress to his burial in Boston.

Afterword

As a boy, John Quincy Adams witnessed a war that led to the birth of a new nation. As a young man, he traveled throughout Europe, gaining a broad view of the world. He began to think about the kinds of improvements he wanted for the new country. Some of these came into being during his lifetime. Most came long after his death.

Today there are observatories or "light-houses of the skies" as he had called them, throughout the country. There are museums like the Smithsonian, universities that teach science, and military academies. There are highways everywhere connecting cities and towns.

The diaries Adams kept throughout his life are fine records of this country's early history. So are his many speeches, essays, and written reports. His poetry reflects his life and times. John Quincy Adams is remembered as a statesman, a scholar, and a poet, just as he hoped he would be.

Bibliography

Bober, Natalie S. *Abigail Adams: Witness to a Revolution.* New York: Atheneum, 1995.

Brookhiser, Richard. *America's First Dynasty: The Adamses, 1735–1918.* New York: The Free Press, 2002.

Adams, Abigail. *The Book of Abigail and John: Selected Letters of the Adams Family, 1762–1784.* Edited by L. H. Butterfield, Marc Friedlaender, and Mary-Jo Kline, Cambridge, MA: Harvard University Press, 1975.

Falkner, Leonard. *The President Who Wouldn't Retire: John Quincy Adams, Congressman from Massachusetts.* New York: Coward-McCann, 1967.

Hecht, Marie B. *John Quincy Adams: A Personal History of an Independent Man.* New York: The Macmillan Company, 1972.

McCullough, David. *John Adams.* New York: Simon & Schuster, 2001.

Nagel, Paul C. *John Quincy Adams: A Public Life, A Private Life.* New York: Alfred A. Knopf, 1997.

Russell, Francis. *Adams: An American Dynasty.* New York: American Heritage Publishing Company, 1976.

Shepherd, Jack. *Cannibals of the Heart: A Personal Biography of Louisa Catherine and John Quincy Adams.* New York: McGraw-Hill, 1980.

Index

Adams, Abigail (mother), 7–9, 15 16, 20, 23, 25, 34; death, 43; relationship with Louisa Johnson, 31, 42

Adams, Abigail "Nabby" (sister) 9, 20

Adams, Charles (brother), 9, 15–17

Adams, Charles Francis (son), 35–36, 38, 52

Adams, children of (all), 30, 35–36, 38

Adams, George Washington (son), 30, 35, 39, 42; death, 51

Adams, John II (son), 33; death 54

Adams, John Quincy: birth, 9; childhood, 7–18; criticism of, 33, 48, 55; death, 59; defending Africans in the Supreme Court, 56; disappointments of, 44; education, 9, 12, 14, 16, 18, 20, 22–23; European travels of, 11–12, 15–18, 21, 31, 36, 38, 42; and the gag rule, 55; grandchildren of, 58; as a lawyer, 23, 26, 32, 56; marriage of, 28–30; and personal loss, 36, 43, 51, 54; as a politician, 27–28, 30–31, 32–36, 38, 40–45, 52, 54–59; as president, 45–50, 52; as a

professor, 34–36; on slavery, 55–58; and treaties, 38, 42; work with weights and measures, 43; writings of, 25–26, 39, 50–51, 58

Adams, Louisa Johnson (wife), 28, 31, 36, 38, 42, 45, 48, 50–52, 54, 58–59

Adams, Louisa Catherine (daughter), 36

Adams, president and vice-president John (father), 8–15, 18–20, 23, 25, 31, 34, 42, 43, 46; death, 48; as president 28–30

Adams, Thomas (brother), 9, 28

Alexander, Czar, 36

Amistad, La, 56

Amsterdam, 16

Battle of Bunker Hill, 7

Boston, MA, 10, 59

Boston, the, 11

Braintree, MA, See Quincy, MA,

Catherine the Great, 17–18

Clay, Henry, 46, 59

Colonial War, 7, 16

Congress, 46, 48–50, 54–55, 59

Continental Congress, 8, 10

Cranch, Billy (cousin), 23

Cranch, Mary (aunt), 21

Crawford, William, 46

Dana, Francis 17
Declaration of Independence, 10, 49, 55, 58
Democratic Party, 49
Department of the Interior, 46

Federalists, 25
France, 11, 14
Franklin, Benjamin, 14

Germany 17–18

Harvard College, 20, 22, 34–36, 42
Haverhill, MA, 22
House of Representatives, 46, 52, 58–59

Jackson, Andrew, 45, 50
Jefferson, President Thomas 10, 30, 48
Johnson, Joshua 28

King Frederick William III, 30
King George III, 8

Letters of Publicola, 25
Louisiana Purchase, 34

Madison, President James, 36, 38
Marcellus, 26
Mende Africans, 56
Monroe Doctrine, 44
Monroe, President James, 40, 42

Natural Philosophy Club, 32
Neva River, 36
Newburyport, MA, 23, 55

Parsons, Theophilus, 23
Penn's Hill, 7
Philidelphia, PA, 8, 14
Potomac River, 43
Princess Elizabeth, 36

Quincy, MA, 7, 10, 34, 42, 48

Republicans, 25

Saint Petersburg, Russia, 36
Shaw, Elizabeth (aunt), 22
Shaw, John (uncle), 22
slavery, 55–58
Smithson, James, 54
Smithsonian Institution, 54
St. Petersburg, Russia, 17
Supreme Court, 56

tariff, or tax bill, 49
Thaxter, John (cousin), 16, 9
Treaty of Paris, 18

University of Leyden, 16, 20

War of 1812, 38
Washington, D.C., 33
Washington, president George, 25
Willard, Joseph, 22

About the Author

In the years since **Beverly Gherman** began writing biographies, she has found more and more children reading them. Recently, after a school visit, a fifth grade student wrote her to say that she originally wanted to become a doctor but after hearing about the pleasure Gherman has writing biographies, she decided she wanted to become a biographer too.

Gherman hopes to continue writing about unique people and sharing their stories with young people, even if that means competition from them in the future. She lives in San Francisco, CA.

About the Illustrator

Matthew Bird was born and raised in Maryland where he learned to love the arts from an early age. He graduated with honors from Pratt Institute and returned to Baltimore where he now works as a freelance illustrator and graphic designer. Although he has done many kinds of work, such as editorial, greeting cards, and portraiture, Matthew most enjoys illustrating children's books. The mediums in creating his art are varied, but he primarily uses watercolor and acrylic paints. "I've been given a wonderful talent and been blessed with the opportunities to do what I love while sharing that gift with others. I can think of no better way to live."

J B ADAMS

**Gherman, Beverly.
First son and
president**

SOF

R4002860008

SOUTH FULTON BRANCH
Atlanta-Fulton Public Library